Edgar Johnson Goodspeed

Funeral Discourse on the Death of Abraham Lincoln

Edgar Johnson Goodspeed

Funeral Discourse on the Death of Abraham Lincoln

ISBN/EAN: 9783337388690

Printed in Europe, USA, Canada, Australia, Japan

Cover: Foto ©ninafisch / pixelio.de

More available books at **www.hansebooks.com**

FUNERAL DISCOURSE

ON THE

DEATH OF ABRAHAM LINCOLN,

PREACHED SUNDAY, APRIL 23RD, 1865,

IN THE

SECOND BAPTIST CHURCH, CHICAGO.

BY REV. E. J. GOODSPEED,

PASTOR.

"HOW ARE THE MIGHTY FALLEN!"

CHICAGO:
PUBLISHED BY THE TRUSTEES.
1865.

CHURCH, GOODMAN & DONNELLEY, PRINTERS, 51 & 53 LA SALLE ST., CHICAGO.

FUNERAL DISCOURSE

DEATH OF ABRAHAM LINCOLN.

WHEN the tidings of President LINCOLN'S assassination threw a gloom over all hearts, Chicago, the metropolis of his State, where he was first nominated for the Presidency, felt especially afflicted. The whole city was draped. The edifice of the Second Baptist Church was very solemnly and appropriately decorated. Two days after the murder, Sabbath, April 16th—a day never to be forgotten—the vast audience melted into tears while the Pastor read David's "lamentation over Saul and Jonathan," 2 Sam. i. 17-27—"*The beauty of Israel is slain upon thy high places; how are the mighty fallen.*" On the Wednesday following, a service was held, in accordance with suggestions from Washington, at which several addresses were made by members of the congregation and others. On Sabbath morning, April 23rd, the Pastor preached a sermon for the occasion to a crowded congregation. A hymn was sung, written by Hon. E. Bixby, which is printed with the discourse. The singing was solemn and impressive, and the whole service was one of deep interest. In the evening, previous to the doxology, Hon. C. C. P. Holden rose and offered a resolution, which was cordially received by the large assembly, that an account of the exercises be preserved in printed form as a memento, and that the Pastor furnish the Trustees with a copy of the sermon preached by him on the death of President LINCOLN. The discourse is here printed precisely as preached.

HYMN.

TUNE—"PLEYEL'S HYMN."

*Written for and sung by the Choir and Congregation of the Second
Baptist Church, April 23rd, 1865.*

Why this grief? this anguish why?
That each breeze is bearing by
'Tis the nation's wail of woe
That our Chief has fallen low

Wise and patient, kind and true,
Savior of his country too;
Love of all the good he won:
He shall live with Washington.

Fallen, not as golden grain,
Gathered on the harvest plain!
Yet the reaper, when he came,
Found him trusting in God's name.

Stricken by the cursed hand
That has blood-stained all our land!
Though defiant man may smite,
God is just, His ways are right!

God of wisdom, love and power,
Keep us in this fearful hour!
Soon may war's dread carnage end,
To us peace with justice send.

SERMON.

THE crime that has bereaved a nation, as if a *Father* had been struck down by the assassin's hand, has but one parallel in history. Another patriot states-man, the idol and hope and leader of his people, in whose nature were harmoniously blended those gen-tle, manly and popular qualities which endeared our own lamented President to so many hearts; in the midst of his years, full of vigor and hope, after fierce and bloody struggles that seemed drawing to a triumphant close, was murdered by a fanatic, in the presence of his family, and died immediately, ex-claiming, "God have mercy on my soul—God have mercy on this poor people."

As our deceased Chieftain treated the assassin kindly but an hour before the fatal wound was given, recognizing him with a genial smile, William of Orange received into his bed-chamber and supplied with money the ruffian who, a few hours after, shot his benefactor with the weapon purchased by that money.

As the assassination that robbed the Netherlands of the wisest, purest and most reliable patriot that had ever lived among men, was suggested and abet-ted by the Spanish authorities who offered rewards for the life of Orange, and encouraged the murderer

in his crime, I believe the wretch who foully slew
our magnanimous, incorruptible and idolized Chief·
Magistrate was spurred and prompted to his plot,
and aided in its execution by the Confederacy whose
treachery and malignity, baffled in the attempt to
take a *nation's* life, fiendishly sought to strike the
constituted' *head,* whose sagacity, firmness, honesty,
courage and wisdom, under God, had thwarted their
purpose. Thanks be to God that this is the last
thrust of the monster's sting ! We have felt it more
keenly than every other. When Sumter fell, and
the flag—symbol of our national honor and greatness
and power—was torn and trodden by rebel hate;
when Ellsworth, gallant and chivalrous as knight of
old, was shot with the starry banner around him by
a desperate ruffian ; when the nation's defenders,
hastening to the national capital to save it from the
enemy, were assaulted by a mob in Baltimore, and
the first blood was shed ; when traitors developed
themselves at the centre of government, and the
crater of treason opened wider and wider at the
foundations of the Temple of Liberty, till all seemed
ready to be engulfed and buried for ever ; when the
first great disasters of the war burst upon us like the
lightnings of divine wrath, that threatened to shiver
the fabric of free government and bury us all in its
ruins ; when one grand event followed another,
bringing tidings of carnage, desolation and wo, our
hearts sunk within us, and we suffered a long agony
of grief. The night was disappearing. The stars of
promise were fading out in the glad light of the
morning. When Charleston fell, the sun appeared,

and we rapturously greeted the golden rim that rose
above the horizon. When Richmond, the cradle of
secession and the den of rebellion, was purged, and
Lee had surrendered, the orb of day broke full and
clear into our sky, and woke everywhere the song of
jubilee. There was scarce a limit to our joy and
hope. The flying Lucifer of revolt might screech
and shriek in helpless wrath, "We will never sur-
render." Yet this only excited our merriment and
pity. We were brimming with confidence that the
glorious end was at hand.

A distinguished company had proceeded to
Charleston to raise over the battered fortress the
banner that there first had been lowered to traitors.
We all rejoiced that he who had held the helm
through the storm was to guide the ship into the
haven of peace amidst the acclamations of a grateful
people. We had trembled for his life as he accom-
panied our victorious army into the Confederate
Capital, and dictated his messages from the chair
defiled by the arch traitor who had plotted his des-
truction and the ruin of his country. We breathed
freer when the tidings flashed across the land that
he was once more safely established in his own home.

It was our settled conviction that he was to live to
behold his country restored, and his own policy vindicated. One enemy after another had ceased to
traduce his name or challenge his prudence. Abused
as no man since Washington was ever abused—the
target of malice and ignorance from extremists of all
parties and sections; denounced as a tyrant, and
pitied as a weak tool of demagogues, or the subject

of womanly tenderness, unbecoming the ruler of a
nation engaged in a stern struggle for life, he was
fast gaining the esteem and trust of all people who
loved liberty throughout the world.

We said he is God's chosen instrument to reconcile
the conflicting elements, to allay animosities, to restore peace and tranquility, and save us from foreign
war. As our venerable Secretary of State was likely
to be removed from life, or from service at least, we
gravitated trustingly and gratefully to the Patriot
and Chieftain who seemed invulnerable and infallible.

At this exultant moment, when the heart of the
nation beat high with gladness and expectation, Oh!
what a blow came crashing through our sensibilities,
our affections, and our sympathies! It was too horrible to be credited! But the information proceeded
from a source that forbade doubt. The incidents
were circumstantially related. Our President was
brutally murdered, and the assassin was at large.
Over all good men there fell a sickening horror.
Business ceased. We were paralyzed by the shock,
and sunk under our burden of woe. Rage was swal-
lowed up in grief. The deed was done, the mischief
accomplished, and the death of the murderer would
not bring back our honored dead or heal the nation's
wo. Men said they had sooner spared any member
of their family. It was a *heart*-grief that smote
them.

Our Friend, in whom our country was incarnate,
the savior of our heritage, and the hope of our future
as citizens of the Republic, lies weltering in his
blood; and we cannot be comforted! As Robert

Hall said at the funeral of the Princess Charlotte :
" An unexampled depopulation of the species by the
sword had indeed nearly rendered death the most
familiar of all spectacles, and left few families unbe-
reaved ; but neither the narrative of battles nor the
sight of carnage are best suited to inculcate the lessons
of mortality ; nor are the moral features of that last
enemy ever less distinctly discerned than in the
moment when he is most busy, or in those fields of
slaughter where he appears the principal agent. The
pomp and circumstance of war, the tumultuous emo-
tions of the combatants, and the eager anxiety of the
contending parties attentive to the important political consequences attached to victory and defeat,
absorb every other impression, and obstruct the
entrance of serious and pensive reflection. How
different the example of mortality presented on the
present occasion! Without the slightest warning,
without the opportunity of a moment's immediate
preparation, in the midst of the deepest tranquility,
at midnight, a voice was heard in the palace, not of
singing men and singing women, not of revelry and
mirth, but the cry, 'Behold, the Bridegroom cometh.'
The mother in the bloom of youth, spared just long
enough to hear the tidings of her infant's death,
almost immediately, as if summoned by his spirit,
follows him into eternity. 'It is a night much to be
remembered.' Who foretold this event? Who con-
jectured it? Who detected at a distance the faintest
presage of its approach, which, when it arrived,
mocked the efforts of human skill, as much by their
incapacity to prevent, as their inability to foresee it!

Unmoved by the tears of conjugal affection, unawed by the presence of grandeur and the prerogatives of power, inexorable death hastened to execute his stern commission, leaving nothing to royalty itself but to retire and weep. Who can fail on this awful occasion to discern the hand of Him, ' Who bringeth princes to nothing, who maketh the judges of the earth as vanity ; who says they shall not be planted ; yea, they shall not be sown ; yea, their stock shall not take root in the earth ; and he shall blow upon them, and they shall wither, and the whirlwind shall take them away as stubble.'

" 'It is better,' says Solomon, ' to go to the house of mourning than to the house of feasting, for that is the end of all men, and the living will lay it to heart'.

" While there are few who are not, at some season or other, conducted to that house, a nation enters it on the present visitation, there to learn, in the sudden extinction of the heiress of her monarchy, the vanity of all but what relates to eternity, and the absolute necessity of having our loins girt, our lamps burning, and ourselves as those who are looking for the coming of the bridegroom."

Shall not *we*, members of the *American* nation, to whom God has now spoken in tones more deep and solemn than on any other occasion, lay to heart the lesson of our mortality ? We must die. The manner, the surroundings, the time of our decease, we cannot know ; therefore, be *ever* in an attitude of expectation, in a state of preparation, by firm habitual reliance on the mercy of our Savior, Jesus Christ.

In common with many others, we felt it to be an aggravation of the sorrow that lacerated our hearts, that our honored Father should have received his fatal wound *in a theatre,* and at the hands of *an actor.* Sustained by the prayers and sympathies and ardent cooperation of that class of community who regard theatres as royal roads to perdition, gilded snares of virtue and manhood, pitfalls where youthful feet stumble into vice, and crime, and ruin; he, whose example was a power and carried tremendous influence—we say it sorrowfully, and only because duty requires the testimony—should never have given them countenance or patronage. In that school men are trained for villainy or nurtured in vice. The honorable exceptions are few in which we find persons attached to theatres who would be considered suitable companions for our children, or visitors at our homes. There is a taint upon them which we shun like the plague. Piety and true excellence are not encouraged by the associations of the play house.

It remained for an actor to reach the lowest hell of crime, in plotting murders that should have throttled the nation; cut every arm of its executive authority; removed the leader of our armies, and struck down men who could have met and mastered the emergency.

It was not a slaveholder who performed this execrable deed, and planned the whole diabolical scheme. The spirit of slavery is selfishness, that developes into lust and cruelty and every conceivable iniquity. We have always apprehended such mani-

festations, and often trembled for the life of our
President. But slavery with its fascinations, peculiarly powerful over such a mind as that of the
assassin, who was born and raised in a slave state—
slavery with its abundant wealth, leisure, aristocracy,
pretense and indulgences of every kind, poisoned the
actor's nature. Familiar with tragedies where the
dagger and poison played important parts, intoxi-
cated by a vain ambition which the theatre fosters,
he was ripe for any crime which might be suggested.
If he had found his noble victim in the house of
God, in the executive mansion, in the capitol, on the
street or in discharge of his official duties, we should
have felt the stroke less severely—one bitter ingre-
dient in our cup would have been wanting.

The nation is humiliated—first by the traitorous
conduct of rebels, then by the sympathizing spirit of
a portion of its citizens who wink at treason, and
lastly by the murder of its President in a theatre by
an actor! What must mankind think of such a
people? How should we hide our heads in shame,
and rise up to wipe away the dishonor by repentance and universal turning unto God.

One thought has been driven deeply—go not to
any place where you would not wish to be found by
death. When inclined to turn aside into a doubtful
path, think whether you would like to be discovered
in that situation dead. I dismiss this point with the
expression of a renewed determination to give no
encouragement henceforth to theatres.

Recurring to the parallel instituted at the outset,
between the crimes which wrapped the Netherlands

in gloom, and threw a whole people into mourning, and that whose keen edge has severed our hopes and laid them low; we read in history that the assassin of Orange was captured, and subjected forthwith to the most excruciating tortures by the magistrates who shared the fury of the populace. Day after day he was put upon the rack, and finally "it was decreed that his right hand should be burned off with a red hot iron, that his flesh should be torn from his bones with pincers in six different places, that he should be quartered and disembowelled alive, that his heart should be torn from his bosom and flung in his face, and that finally his head should be taken off." The execution of this awful sentence occurred in all its horrors, in presence of the multitude who applauded the deed. That was vengeance. But the historian has pronounced it unjustifiable under the most aggravating circumstances, and no one approves it who possesses the humane spirit of christianity. The criminal's agonies could not restore life to the murdered prince, nor confer honor upon his memory. Brutality could not accomplish the ends of justice, since it demoralized the popular conscience, and roused the fury of the enemy who sought satisfaction in blood for the sufferings of their hired assassin. Vengeance kindles all the malicious passions into a blaze, and provokes to the commission of new and greater crimes. Revenge has wasted nations, whelming lives and fortunes, homes and treasures in one grave. Retaliation often defeats the highest ends of justice, and dethrones reason and right, setting up mad fury in their stead, which leads to extremes that curse and destroy man's best interests, while God is unheeded and dishonored.

Abraham LINCOLN was right, and deserves the praise of all men for his unswerving observance of the humane principles of the New Testament; for his leniency towards offenders; for his genial commiseration of the errors and crimes of rebels; for his adherence to a policy which has saved the country from being demoralized in the midst of civil war; which has taken from the foe every just cause of complaint, made their epithets of "tyrant" and "butcher" heaped on his name, the ridicule of the world, and given us a moral ascendancy more brilliant than military renown.

The heart of our people has beat tenderly towards the enemy. Throughout the war we have exhibited no malice or malignity. The bitterness and rage expressed by their ferocious conduct, have only provoked our pity and scorn, while we sate in our quietness and prosperity at home, or met them face to face on the sanguinary field. Hence the war has not degraded the loyal North, but rather elevated the tone of public sentiment, and educated us in all nobleness and beneficence.

We were ready to forgive these misguided people in revolt, and extend them every generous and righteous privilege. We saw their towns burned, their plantations wasted, the beauty and glory of the land withered and tarnished, their wealth destroyed, their pride humbled, their young men smitten, and, above all, their favorite institution, like Dagon, beheaded before the ark of God. We said

it is enough. God has visited upon them wrath
without measure. In our triumph we were disposed
to a lenity that was in danger of trenching on justice.
Those haughty, cunning lords of the South, before
whom Northern men have too often bent the syco-
phantic knee, were ready to step once more into their
old places of power, and recommence their conniv-
ances and chicanery. Justice was likely to lose its
rights; and justice has its place in human govern-
ments and in the divine administration as well as
mercy. He who had so far wisely conducted us and
well, tempering sternness and severity with mildness
and humanity, had done his work. He dies, lamented
by millions, as no man was ever mourned since time
began, and leaves a record pure and bright as any
that history bears, and becomes the sublime inheritance of the American Republic to remotest generations. The hand of secession strikes him down and
maddens the nation. The enemy of God and of man
seals its own doom and leads upon the stage one who
has learned its nature by personal contact with
slavery and the rebel chiefs, who knows how to deal
with it as it inherently deserves, and who has demonstrated his courage and his purpose in earnest words
and heroic deeds. And yet he is but a man—
encompassed, as we have been painfully taught, by
infirmity—and as such he needs our prayers and wise
counsels and faithful cooperation.

Moses, with all his great qualities and endowments,
did not seem to be the appropriate instrument with
which God would chastise the idolatrous Canaanites,
and he was laid aside by the divine decree when his

eyes had caught the glories of the Promised Land.
The work of justice, involving war and desolation,
was committed to Joshua, in whose hands the sword
was more firmly grasped and vigorously wielded.
God, "Who executeth all things after the counsels
of His own will," has permitted the painful event
which prostrated our Moses, and introduced into
power our Joshua. He will be immortal till his work
is done. His mission ended, he will be compelled to
make room for another, till all the purposes of
heaven are accomplished on earth. "The Lord
reigneth, let the earth rejoice." For "He doeth all
things well." Only let individuals and nations see
to it that they run not counter to omnipotent justice;
that they harmoniously co-work with Him who
causeth all things to work together for good to them
that love Him.

In the review of our estimate and treatment of the
honored dead, we see, perhaps, how grossly we mis-
judged, how cruelly we maligned, how hastily we
condemned, how blindly we murmured. It required
all the exertions of calm, candid, thoughtful men to
restrain the heated impatience and correct the false
judgments which cast their long, black shadows
across the land. Time has vindicated him whom
God was leading in accordance with our prayers.
My heart often ached when men by tongue and pen
were depreciating and reviling the great and good
man. I thank God that in all my prayers and
remarks and influences, during both terms of his
office, I ever stood by him unfalteringly, and
defended and maintained him against all manner of

aspersion. No word of censure fell from these lips upon the head or heart of this man. What an example did he himself leave behind of considerate charity. In his messages and speeches, who discovers aught that argues pride or malice, intolerance or selfwill? That late inaugural breathes the very soul of Christianity, and would seem to have been written within sound of the Savior's dying prayer: "Fondly do we hope, fervently do we pray that this mighty scourge of war may speedily pass away. Yet if it be God's will that it continue until the wealth piled by bondmen by two hundred and fifty years' unrequited toil shall be sunk, or until every drop of blood drawn with the lash shall be repaid by another drawn with the sword, as was said three thousand years ago, so still it must be said that the judgments of the Lord are true and righteous altogether. With malice towards none, with charity for all, with firmness for the right as God gives us to see the right, let us strive on to finish the work we are in, to bind up the nation's wounds, to care for those who shall have borne the battle, and for their widows and orphans. And with all this, let us strive after a just and lasting peace among ourselves and with all nations."

These solemn words were utterances of the heart. We shall mourn most suitably and effectively, and acceptably to God, if we learn by our experience with ABRAHAM LINCOLN, that tolerance, charity, moderation, patience and trust in truth and God, which he exhibited during his Presidential career.

As our country has not yet emerged from the diffi-

2

culties originated by secession; as the new Chief
Magistrate is called to a post glorified by his prede-
cessor, a position of tremendous responsibility and
hazard, as we cannot measure the situation nor
realize all the conflicting interests that gather about
him, and as we have been taught the fallibility of
human judgment by our past experience, may we
practice towards ANDREW JOHNSON that candor,
patience, moderation and considerateness, which
reason and christianity suggest. In our haste we
have already done him wrong, and prayed that he
might never take the chair of state. God has rebuked
our error, and once more reminded us that we should
ever pray, "Thy will be done." Yet have we been
instructed by his misstep : that in the Unchangeable
Ruler alone can we infallibly trust." "It is not in
man that walketh to direct his steps." May the
mantle of the ascended chief fall on his successor,
and the wisdom of God be our salvation!

The death of our President seemed peculiarly un-
timely—a kind of mockery of human life. With his
blood God has written in broad characters upon all
things earthly, "vanity"—"emptiness"—"disappoint-
ment." We are so easily crazed by prosperity, that
mankind idolize success. Had President LINCOLN
failed through unavoidable circumstances, his name
would not have been revered as now. Had he lived
to see the triumphant termination of the struggle,
and the restoration of law and order, with universal
freedom, and sunk to rest at a good old age, crowned
with the love of a generous people, we should have
recognized less clearly the need of divine grace and

salvation to a perfect life.   Now again the lesson is
repeated, that men were not created to find their rest
and perfection here.   A miscreant, living in de-
bauchery, baying the government that shielded him,
was able to destroy that living combination of *good-
ness* and *power* which made Mr. LINCOLN a *great*
man; to cut him off from the attainment of the prize
that gleamed just before him in his upward career;
to plunge the nation into profoundest grief; to
change the policy of a mighty people, and perhaps
the destiny of millions; and to demonstrate by what
a slender thread are suspended all things dear to man.

To those who study the nature and consequences
of sin, this furnishes another illustration of the possible evils that lie in germ within man's fallen nature;
another exemplification of the power of depravity;
a proof of the justice of God in forever excluding
unregenerate sinners from the abode of the righteous
in glory; and an incitement to humble, unceasing
prayer that we may be kept, purified, sanctified and
made meet for the inheritance of the saints in light.
Let us rest in the assurance that though he who perpetrated the deed may possibly escape human justice,
divine wrath will pursue him to his remotest hiding
place.   "The wicked shall not go unpunished."
"Vengeance is mine, I will repay, saith the Lord."
Much as I loved and honored him who was foully
slain by a wretch that deserves no breath of air or
breadth of space anywhere out of the bottomless pit,
I still would not personally harm him, except in self-
defense, or as an officer of the law, clothed with its
authority, and burdened with the responsibility of

executing justice and maintaining order. Such, could he return to life by a miracle of divine love, would be the feeling of that kind man who sleeps, alas! the sleep that knows no waking. The idea of vengeance should be carefully excluded from every mind, and the spirit of revenge from all hearts. We may cry to God for justice, we may appeal to our magistrates for justice, but remembering that we too are sinners, that fortuitous events gave us birth in the North and determined our creed, that our late lamented President, in the spirit of Jesus, counselled moderation and clemency, let us show the deeds of mercy, and · push on the car of civilization to new elevations of humanity and Christ-like love. Let us not push it back into the old ruts of retaliation, persecution and barbarism. In the changeful affairs of this world the party in power becomes the minority, and is compelled to drink the cup it mixed for others. We may possibly be mingling a draught for the enemy now under our feet, that will afterwards be commended to the lips of our children. We shall be cautious what ingredients we infuse. There is no millennium at hand, so far as human vision can read the signs of the times. The more of christianity we can diffuse—of pure New Testament charity and truth—the more hope for our race, the greater glory for ourselves with Him whose praise and rewards outweigh earthly fame and compensation as the universe surpasses an atom.

It is not for me to say what should be done with the men of the South. But as for slavery, *their* curse and ours—a wrong and an evil which oppresses millions of men as deserving of freedom as ourselves, nurses barbarism, and subjects the whole nature and resources of men to selfishness, I would have it extirpated root and branch, till every man is as free by birth, in the eye of the law, as in the sight of his Maker. I would have every avenue of improvement opened to all men without distinction. I would have schools and colleges and churches multiplied over the whole land. I would have the ballot box untrammelled, and compel the people who have means to feel the necessity of educating and developing every man, because he has a vote and exerts an influence on the affairs of his country. To all I would add as the *essential saving* accompaniment a free Gospel, which the South has not had, preached in love and power, without let or hindrance, to all inhabitants of the land. We have lost two former Presidents; but our country was not lost, because "the Eternal God is our refuge." He planted religion and liberty on these shores, and has guarded and nurtured them through wars and trials. To Him we owe the noble men who rocked the cradle of Independence, and cemented the foundations of Christian faith. For all our prosperity and the blessings that make us a happy people, we give thanks to God. And we *glorify Him* in our mention of the virtues and excellencies, the sayings and acts of the mighty dead. The life and character of President LINCOLN have become familiar themes which our poor pen can no further illustrate or adorn. You know the story of his life from year to year. The sturdy physical frame, untouched by disease, the genial good nature, the large tender heart, the broad

practical comprehensive mind, the patient candor,
the generous enthusiasm, the cheerful courage, the
invincible honesty, the earnest trust in God, and the
wise reliance on the people, have been illuminated,
and are known by heart. The distant historian, with
larger acquaintance with secret information and rebel
history, and looking at the mature *results* of his policy
and character, will correct some of our judgments,
but detract nothing from the splendor of his fame.
Another name is added to the roll of great men
which we proudly contemplate and regard among our
treasures.   It cannot be doubted that men will ever
speak of him as next to the first Father of his
country in his claim on the reverence and affection of
the American people.   And even the descendants of
the rebel South will learn that the bullet which
sought his life, slew their truest, safest friend.   For
he conceived that fidelity to his country was consis-
tent with clemency and justice towards his infatuated
foes.   The race to whom he gave liberty, for whom
he prepared a path to manhood, will cherish his
memory with sacred enthusiasm, and aid in building
high and enduring his monument.   " A great, a good
and a right mind," said the old Roman Seneca, "is a
kind of divinity lodged in flesh ; it came from heaven
and to heaven it must return."   While his dust
claims our honors as it passes on to its last resting
place, and the solemn pageant preaches of mortality
and of sin's ruin, the soul that informed it reposes in
the light of that countenance to which it was wont
to be upturned in daily prayer.   Freed from the
anxiety, the temptation, responsibility, care, fatigue,

fear and sin of earth, the immortal spirit shines, through the grace of Christ, " a star of day." Let this remind us that there is a life for man, in which the infinite perfections of spiritual being allure not to disappoint, where aspirations that know no limit shall be satisfied forever in the love of God.

And now, friends, from the shattered image, majestic in the ruin which sin wrought and Providence repaired, from the creature, whose greatness is but a shadow of the Infinite, turn we to the Creator, Immutable and Eternal!

> " Thou art the source and centre of all minds,
>   Their only point of rest, Eternal Word!
> From Thee departing, they are lost, and rove
> At random, without honor, hope or peace.
> From Thee is all that soothes the life of man,
> His high endeavor and his glad success,
> His strength to suffer and his will to serve.
> But oh! thou bounteous Giver of all good,
> Thou art of all Thy gifts Thyself the crown.
> Give what Thou canst, without Thee we are poor,
> And with Thee rich, take what Thou wilt away."

Now unto the King Eternal, Immortal, Invisible, the only Wise God, our Savior, be glory everlasting! Amen!

REST, MARTYR, REST.

BY JAMES G. GLASS.

I.

'Tis finished! On Columbia's head
  Doth gasping Treason pour
Its seventh vial of fiendish wrath!
  Her Father is no more!
The foulest deeds of Treason's life
  Which filled the land with woe:
How vain beside its dying stroke,
  Which lays our Chieftain low.

CHORUS.

Rest, Martyr, rest,
  From the scenes of death and pain,
Though murd'rous hands have stilled thy heart
  Thy noble deeds remain.

II.

Four years as chieftain did he toil
  To free our own fair land,
And traitors all around him stood,
  To grasp it from his hand;
And in our nation's gladdest hour
  The assassin's hand was near;
It struck our noble Lincoln down—
  Columbia's hearts hold dear.

III.

The nation's heart o'erflowed with joy
  To see the conflict cease,
And grim war's bursting clouds revealed
  The angel form of peace.
The Union safe, the slave set free,
  By his kind heart and hand:
Oh! why must he, like Moses, die
  In view of Canaan's land.

IV.

We should not question Providence,
  Who wisely rules o'er all,
And in His tender love doth mark
  The tiny sparrow's fall.
But tremble, traitors, lest the wrath
  Your murd'rous act hath sown,
Leave Justice free from Mercy's prayers
  To deal with you alone.

FAST DAY SERMON.

JUNE 1st, 1865.

UPON earnest assurance that this hasty development of an important truth would do good, and round up this memento of events, solemn and awful beyond all precedent in American history, the author gives it to his congregation of loyal and patriotic men and women who have been behind none in devotion to the Union and its lamented Chieftain; praying that when *our* sin shall find us out, we may stand in the shadow of the Cross of Jesus, who died and ever liveth " to save his people from their sins."

NUMBERS xxxii. 23—" * * And be *sure your sin will find you out.*"

THE sin described by Moses in this threatening was national, or the sin of a people. As a nation is an aggregation of individuals, the declaration couched in the figure is applicable to every human being in his single solitary existence as well as in his associated capacity. "Be sure *your* sin," &c. "God will visit indignation and wrath, &c., upon *every* soul that doeth evil." There is a divine retribution evermore making itself felt in the world—an inevitable punishment for guilty man. The tragic and awful events connected with the rise, progress and overthrow of the Southern rebellion will not leave us wise unless we learn from them this great and momentous truth.

1. The Divine Word bears in flaming characters on its portals, "He will by no means spare the guilty." As we enter and traverse the temple of inspiration, we read the same announcement in various forms. And the explicit doctrine finds ample illustration in historic pictures, which mutually explain each other. "The Lord thy God is a jealous God" written over Nebuchadnezzar's portrait sketched by Daniel, pours a flood of light on the prophet's work, which in turn reflects it on the Mosaic declaration. "Be sure your sin will find you out" is interpreted by the experience of Joseph's brethren when they trembled beneath the frown of the unknown stranger at Pharaoh's court. Like a hound pursuing the prey, though long baffled or dallying with the victim till the master shall slip the leash, vengeance followed them to the brink of ruin, and sprang on them there in the hour of direst extremity. The canvas that bears the outline of Herod's bloody career and terrible death is surrounded as with flaming torches by such texts as these: "Evil pursueth sinners." "Woe unto the wicked ; it shall be ill with him. For the reward of his hands shall be given him." "Our God is a consuming fire." "Vengeance is mine, I will repay, saith the Lord."

It seemed a strange thing for Jesus to sit down upon the Mount of Olives and contemplate Jerusalem, till tears started from his eyes and stole down his cheeks, as he predicted the consequences of her sin in rejecting the Messiah ; and more pathetic still for him to say to the Jewish women that bewailed his wretchedness and woe as he staggered towards

Calvary, bleeding and suffering, "Weep not for me, but weep rather for yourselves and for your children." His prophecies were "idle tales" to the proud leaders and their deluded followers. But their sin found them out, and was described to them in language not to be misunderstood, as they and their children perished and their city disappeared in fire and desolation. " There is a God who judgeth in the earth;" and "He will bring to light the hidden things of darkness;" and "The wheat will he gather into his garner, but the chaff will he burn with unquenchable fire."

2. The idea of a divine retribution pursuing sinners relentlessly, and inevitably bringing them to justice soon or late, seems to be interwoven with the consciousness of man. Like a thread deeply dyed, it appears everywhere running through all history, religions, languages and forms of speech. The better days of heathenism had a Nemesis or goddess of vengeance, who never failed, however slowly she seemed to move, to appear at the opportune moment to punish crime. Her office affords a perfect illustration of the text. The criminal might think his deed unobserved, and congratulate himself on having escaped detection, and provided surely against it; but the keen-eyed divinity, tracking the perpetrator long and surely, removed at last the veil, exposed him, and invoked justice on his guilty head.

There was a proverb in ancient Greece—"The cranes of Ibycus," which expressed the prevailing sense of the age. Ibycus was robbed and murdered in a lonely spot. A flock of cranes were observed sailing above their heads as the villains finished their work. Time passed on. These murderers were sitting in the open theatre without roof, in Athens, and saw a flock of cranes hovering over the city. They said among themselves, " Behold the avengers of Ibycus." The remark was caught up by one who sat near. They were arrested, confessed the crime, and were put to death. Hence the proverb.

All nations and times have similar phrases that unfold the popular faith in a sure retribution. *We* say, " Murder will out." The Greeks said, " Punishment is lame, but it comes." "The mill of God grinds late, but it grinds to powder;" or "The mill of God grinds small, but it grinds all." In these sayings lies the conscious assurance of penalty for evil-doing. " God comes with leaden feet, but strikes with iron hands." The same universal faith growing from conscience, and confirmed by observation and experience takes the form of warning. · " Who sows thorns let him not go unshod." Well would it have been for the rebel chiefs had they suffered the proverb to save them from that sowing which has become to them a bed not of roses, but of thorns sharp as avenging justice can produce to pierce the wickedest criminals.

Humbler proverbs flying about from lip to lip, repeat evermore the solemn assertion of the text. "Ashes always fly back in the face of him that throws them." " Curses, like chickens, always come *home* to roost."

The field of anecdote *abounds* with instances of the almost certain discovery and punishment of crime, under all possible circumstances. History furnishes numberless corroborations of the truth that " God," as one has said, " will not let man alone. When man's passion is strong and bent upon indulgence, avenging justice may seem as if standing aside and inattentive ; but it is only that it may seize him with a more powerful grasp in the state of exhaustion that follows. When the plots of cunning and deceit are successful, it may look as if God did not observe human affairs ; but when the dishonest man is caught at last, he finds it to be in toils which have for years been weaving for him. It not unfrequently happens that every opposing power, which the wicked thinks he has crushed, rises up to pursue and punish him, when the tide of fortune is turning against him. Every drop of that cup of bitter elements which he has been filling for others, he must drink himself, when he has filled up the measure of his iniquities. The fagots which he has been collecting for the des-truction of others all go to augment the flame of his funeral pile. The drunkard is not more certainly haunted by the frightful apparitions called up by the disease which follows excess, than crime is pur-sued by its avenging spirits. There is, if we may so speak, a gathering and closing in at the death, and that to behold his agonies and humiliation, of all the powers which have been in scattered scent and pur-suit of him, throughout the whole hunting grounds of his career. It is affirmed of the drowning man that in the brief space of time that precedes uncon-sciousness, every event of his past life passes in rapid review before his eyes ; and there is certainly something of this hurrying in the avenging events, all having a connexion with his past life, which God crowds on one another, to make the ambitious, the proud and malignant discover that He has all along been ruling their destiny."

No more notable and perfect example of this has been brought forth on the stage by poet or historian than God himself now presents to the scornful gaze of mankind.

An intensely proud man, leader of a class who vaunted themselves in aristocracy, chivalry, and all these excrescences of human pride, who lorded it over his peers in the Senate of his country, and threatened dreadful deeds if his views and purposes were voted down by the nation, who actually forsook his seat, turned away with curses from the Capitol that enshrined a nation's glory and sovereignty, and waged war on the government of his fathers, which had given him and them peace, wealth and honor—returns to that Capitol a fettered, execrated, fallen wretch, laden with crimes too appalling for pen to describe or tongue to utter, humiliated by disasters more overwhelming than ever befel a rebellion, and disgraced by personal cowardice that led him to shun honorable, manly death in the last ditch, for attempted flight in the habiliments of a woman. Has not Providence demonstrated Himself in this accumulation of mortifying and painful events upon the Chief of the Confederacy? What human ingenuity could have arranged for such a fall and humiliation? The capital gone, the armies melted, the country a waste, the navy surrendered, the leader in irons—

with the horrible guilt of complicity in our President's assassination fastened on them, their people disgusted with them, and hungry, and ragged, and beaten utterly; their cities ravaged by fire and decimated by explosions; the world deserting and scoffing at them, while the flag they trampled and defied, shines in new richness and beauty, known and honored throughout the earth; the people they scorned, are pronounced the bravest soldiers in the world; the cities they threatened, are stretching out their hands to grasp the wealth of all nations; the fields they would ravage wave in luxuriant promise of unequalled harvests, while religion and education shed their blessings in unstinted profusion among a happy, prosperous people, whom he sought to humble and destroy. Does history show any thing like it? Could our text have a more apt or impressive interpretation? And when at length justice shall have had its righteous sway, we may repeat the stirring passage in Mr. Reed's poem of Tuesday, with sad, yet more satisfactory exultation.

> " Once more within this marvelous Temple here,
> Let us exult o'er Treason's bloody bier—
> Exult like Miriam on the Red Sea's coast,
> Whose waves uniting drowned old Pharaoh's host.
> The billows of our union thus have met
> And overwhelmed and drowned the traitorous set;
> And Liberty like singing Miriam stands
> With flashing cymbals in her lifted hands,
> Shouting her pæans gladly to the Lord
> For Freedom won and union thus restored."

Can secession and rebellion have any future champions? Will any rash spirits ever dare to attempt the life of this nation? Let them be sure their sin

will find them out. It will find them out as lightning shivers the oak, and leaves nought but splint-
ered fragments and crisped foliage to tell the story
of God's terrible and swift wrath.

Thanks be unto Him who hath caused this
haughty, boastful, insolent, causeless, diabolical confederacy, to meet a ruin, both comical and tragical,
to the last degree. The respect it once had has gone
out like the snuff of a candle. It is a thing of deri-
sion for mankind. How could He who hates slavery
and loves freedom for man, have more effectually dishonored and destroyed the slaveholders' rebellion!
It is not man's work but God's, and to Him be all
the glory.

We contemplate the murder of President LINCOLN
with horror; and yet it is the tacit concession of the
whole people, that this was the bitterest of the dregs
of that cup which God was pressing to the lips of
the South. In it culminated that spirit which has
enslaved, and whipped, and robbed, and outraged
generations of human beings; which griped the
nation's throat, plundered its treasury, and slew
myriads of its best and bravest citizens; which
gagged and flogged, imprisoned, fined and banished,
shot, hunted down with blood hounds, hung by lynch
law, or starved free citizens who loved liberty and
the flag of their fathers, and which treated thousands
of our soldiers captured in war, like beasts and not
like men. This was the climax of iniquity, and men
read in it afresh the malignity and cowardice of aristocracy and chivalry, based on slavery. It is a crime
against humanity, and virtue and love, as embodied

with rare perfection in our honored President. The guilt and stain gave a deeper crimson to the gory dye of the confederacy, and left it without excuse or champion among men. And above all, it placed them in the hands of a sterner magistrate, who bears not the sword in vain. God permitted it for a wise purpose, to bring more dreadful vengeance on the guilty men, who bathed our nation in blood, and well-nigh robbed the human race of its best hopes of political welfare under free institutions. How it united our people—a common sorrow melting them into one brotherhood, and gathering us all at God's mercy seat! It built for the mighty dead a monument in every patriot heart. We forgot every thing but his virtues, and enshrined his memory among our most sacred things. It nerved us up to do justice, to allow the sword of Government to smite where treason invited the avenging blow, and God himself pointed His own finger and said— "strike." We bow under His Divine hand, and say from our hearts—"The Lord God Omnipotent reigneth, let the earth rejoice." "Shall not the Judge of the whole earth do right?"

The text is also verified in the assassin's marvelous career. He was a sinner from his youth up—a gross and reckless gambler and libertine. Petted and flattered, and partially successful, he doubtless felt none of the restraints which dread of Divine retribution imposes. Had he not thus far escaped the supposed evil consequences of his ungodly course, and was there not impunity for him? He scarcely took to heart the experience of so many men like

3

himself, who seldom fail to have foretastes in this life
of the perdition that awaits God's unrepentant enemies. Rebelling against every natural and providen-
tial influence to save him, he was suffered to plunge
on till he came under the power of the temptation to
make way with the President. His arrangements
for the murder and escape were perfected with skill
and promised entire success. The deed was performed and the assassin leaped upon the stage shout-
ing in triumph. But ah! his spur caught in the
folds of the flag and threw him, breaking his limb.
How his well-laid plan was marred and spoiled by
this simple Providence! God so ordered that the
emblem of our national authority, consecrated by
patriot blood, should avenge its dishonor on the perpetrator of the foul crime that lowered it on every
flag-staff over the whole earth where it swayed.
Follow the bloody trail all along, and see how it
involved by one means and another, the whole band
of conspirators. And behold the villain in his lair,
already smitten with death by his agonizing wounds,
before the fatal bullet pierced him. See him writh-
ing in tortures, and to the last, obdurate in his
wicked exultation over the crime. Dying like a dog,
he lies in a nameless grave, forever execrated by all
good men throughout the world. There is no
redeeming feature in the whole transaction. Found
out by his sin, he died as the fool dieth, having no
hope and without God.

We have all suffered and shall suffer to the end of
life, and that because we have sinned and shall sin.
Our case has been illustrated by that of an " individ-

nal who has committed a horrible crime, when intox-
icated, and is committed to prison while yet in a
state of unconsciousness. On awakening to reflection, he would make inquiry in reference to his past
or present state ; but he finds that there is none to
answer him. He utters a cry of alarm or agony,
but no reply is given. He would conclude that he
is abandoned by all ; but on turning round and
round, he finds prison walls, with only so much of
the light of heaven shining through as to show that
pains have been taken to render his escape hopeless.
What other conclusion can he draw than that he is
shut up in prison, awaiting the time when he is to
be brought out to trial?   Does it not seem as if man
was in a somewhat similar position, abandoned and
yet watched, spared in life, but spared as if for trial?
And it were well if, instead of seeking to drown
misery by frantic merriment, or to beat uselessly
against his prison walls, he was endeavoring to
realize the nature and extent of that crime of which
he is but half conscious, and anxiously inquiring if
there be not some way of arresting the judgment
which may soon be pronounced against him."

   Are *we* not summoned to such a course by the
crimes and sufferings of the present time?   The
catalogue of iniquities bears none which has not been
perpetrated in our midst.   The human race knows
no form of woe that has not been realized among
us of late.   God's power and purpose to punish sin
remain the same as when He revealed Himself to
Moses.   Who will not seek to humble his soul under
the mighty hand of God.

If we see any national sin going forward, may we
wash our hands of complicity with it, and strive to
uproot it, lest it court the lightnings of His dis-
pleasure.   Slavery is dead.   Would to God that
intemperance, Sabbath breaking, and other crying
sins were in the grave with it, to know no
resurrection!

Going down into our hearts and searching our
lives, we may find much that dishonors God. "Be
sure your sin will find you out." We cannot bury
our transgressions, nor hide our depravity and
unbelief from the Omniscient. Why should we wish
to do so, unless blinded and infatuated by Satan and
love of evil? God will forgive (and this is like the
rising of the sun after a night of storm and darkness
and terror), God will forgive those who confess
and forsake their sins in the name of Him who "is
able to save them to the uttermost who come unto
God by Him."   This truth relieves God of all
imputations of malice. He is not vindictive. Just
though He is, His justice is love and kindness to the
men who serve him by holiness and benevolence, or
who forsake their folly and wickedness in repentance
and righteousness. The pillar of cloud and of fire
that shone on the Israelites, and guided them, was
darkness and mist to the proud and heathen and
godless oppressor. Jesus himself was severe and
tender, never reckless or malignant. · Men slew him
because they were condemned by his truth and
virtues, as they did ABRAHAM LINCOLN, who loved
righteousness and hated iniquity. Men resist and
hate God who would have all come to repentance

that they may not perish. How vain and futile their rage and opposition! Yesterday, puling in the cradle, to-morrow, rotting in the grave, man wastes himself, as the waves that beat against the ever-lasting cliffs, when he rebels against Omnipotence. "There is no cowardice in capitulating with God." We sacrifice nothing of our dignity. we compromise no principles of manliness or honor, but rather glorify ourselves when we come to God and beg for mercy, and take up our neglected duty.

As "Sin is a reproach to any people and righteous-ness exalteth a nation," may we, in pure love to our country, join those who are leagued to destroy sin, and promote righteousness. Unswervingly true to the God of our fathers, we shall best serve our native land and our common humanity.

Our skies may not always be bright; but the storms that fall will prepare for us new and greater blessings if we remain firm in our allegiance to Heaven's King. The nation will be reconstructed on a firmer basis, with freedom as its corner stone at every corner from ocean to ocean and from the lakes to the Gulf. Our enemies will yet rejoice in the new order of things, and submit to a better condition with patience and wisdom. A free gospel will wake to life and salvation the multitudes that throng our shores from both hemispheres, and "God, even our own God, will bless us!"

www.ingramcontent.com/pod-product-compliance
Lightning Source LLC
Chambersburg PA
CBHW021450090426
42739CB00009B/1697